Shared-Parenting Workbook

Sharing-parenting after Divorce – What is it, how does it work and will it work for you?

Toby Hazlewood

Contents

Foreword 3

Workbook Overview 5

   Introduction 5

   Approach 6

   Context and Definitions 7

   Is it for us? 9

   Golden Rules in Summary 11

Golden Rule #1 14

Golden Rule #2 20

Golden Rule #3 26

Golden Rule #4 30

Golden Rule #5 34

Golden Rule #6 38

Golden Rule #7 42

Golden Rule #8 44

Golden Rule #9 48

Golden Rule #10 51

Golden Rule #11 54

Golden Rule #12 58

Golden Rule #13 61

Golden Rule #14 65

Conclusion 69

Foreword

Thank you for taking the time to pick up this book. I assume that unless you've decided to read it out of pure interest, you are considering divorce or separation from your partner or are already in the midst of the process. Maybe you've been parted for some time and are looking to see how you can improve your life.

 I'm further assuming that you've got kids within that relationship and that as well as weathering the split as best you can, you are most concerned to ensure that once the dust has settled and you and your ex have metaphorically gone your separate ways, you are able to continue to parent your kids as effectively as possible.

You are rightly keen to minimise the impact of your parting upon their happiness and wellbeing, and to ensure that they are not just another product of a broken home, whose family structure has a defining effect on them forever more, for all the wrong reasons.

I know from personal experience that at this time you will be overwhelmed by the vast array of things that need to be sorted, information that needs to be digested, choices that need to be made and arrangements that need to be formulated ranging from the significant (dividing up mutual assets such as houses or pension funds accumulated within the relationship) through to the somewhat trivial division of the consumer goods picked up along the way. I contend though that none of these matters is as important as deciding on how most effectively to raise your kids in the aftermath of your separation and for that reason I want to offer you some reassurance if I can that in picking up this book I think you have made a solid first move.

My name is Toby Hazlewood and what I have to share with you is the lessons I've learned in the last 11+ years of parenting apart from my ex-wife following the break-up of our marriage in 2005. With little in the way of acrimony and two kids borne from our marriage, we determined that the future happiness of our kids was our number one priority and for that reason we decided to explore alternative ways of raising them. In the years that have followed, we've learned a lot, enjoyed plenty of highs and suffered many lows and challenges. But through it all we have maintained a focus on raising our kids as best we could.

If I had been faced with the prospect of some targeted and focussed advice on how to raise kids post-divorce, in a non-traditional parenting model from those that are largely the norm these days, I would have leapt at the chance to take it. There seem to be numerous books and advisers on the legal and financial aspects of divorce and separation, but what this book attempts to do is to focus on the parenting of the kids from failed relationships.

It advocates an approach that is non-typical, but which I contend works, and works well in allowing the needs of the kids and the parents to be met. Done well, I contend it is as-effective (if not more-effective) than raising kids in a traditional relationship; two people who exist in a relationship aren't necessarily guaranteed to make good parents, and it doesn't mean the needs of the kids are always given primary consideration just because the parents remain together.

I could go on further but I know that at present your time and attention are precious and so I'll leave it there. I have a wealth of other content and products to support you on your journey if the content of this initial workbook seems to gel for you. In the meantime, I wish you well and hope that through this book you'll take comfort that everything will be okay for you and your kids.

Toby

Workbook Overview

Introduction

In 2016 I published a book originally written as part of the process of rebuilding my life following divorce from my first wife and the events during the years that followed.

At the dawning of the year 2000 at barely 24 years old I found myself a new parent with a daughter to support in a fledgling relationship with my then girlfriend (of little more than 3 months when we conceived) who would become my eventual wife. Five years later, with a second daughter between us, having shared an eventful few years of marriage we had reached the conclusion that our relationship had reached its natural end and we were going to part albeit on reasonably good terms.

You can read the details behind the founding of the relationship and the subsequent events and circumstances leading to its demise in that book at a future point should you wish, but the significant factor in our split was that we were not content to settle for a conventional set-up as far as our separated family was concerned.

The key message behind that book is that whilst relationships and families break up every day, it doesn't always have to come down to acrimony, custody agreements and disputes over visitation rights when negotiating for the future upbringing of the children of the relationship. There is a way that kids can be raised with the involvement of both Mum and Dad that gives parents and kids alike the best possible family environment that can be established; namely via shared-parenting where each parent fulfils 50% of the parenting role for the kids.

It is just such a structure that we set out to establish as the framework for parenting of our kids, who were 7 and 3 by the time this arrangement was in place. The arrangement has been maintained for many years now, and with the eldest daughter recently turning 17, I feel confident in describing it as successful.

This is not a simple arrangement to establish and it requires considerable forethought, flexibility and resourcefulness in order to make it work. It also demands commitment on behalf of both the parents in both doing what is best for the kids above all else. We had acknowledged the end our relationship as husband and wife, but our relationship as parents to the kids remained and would endure regardless. We determined that it was our priority to give our kids the best possible upbringing as a separated family and I'm assuming that this is your primary aim since you have gone so far as to pick up this book. If I can make it work, then I genuinely believe anyone can.

Often, desire to do or achieve something is completely removed from the realities of whether it will be achievable. I'm painfully aware that when a couple with kids has decided to divorce or separate there are numerous matters requiring careful and meticulous consideration and as such the prospect of wading through a personal and in-depth account of how I established shared-parenting is probably a bit overwhelming and superfluously detailed at this stage.

For this reason I've created a pared-back version of the original book that focusses first and foremost on assisting you to consider whether it is a possibility for you in yours and your families lives; hence the emergence of this book.

Of course, if you arrive at the conclusion it is something you can get value from then the original book and a number of other associated tools and services are there for your use.

When you've decided to part, undoubtedly the first course of sensible action is to consider your options and make some informed choices, just one of which is how to establish a framework for continuing to raise your kids.

Approach
The purpose of this book is to distil the knowledge from my original book with lighter associated narrative and background surrounding my circumstances, by focussing on the pre-existing conditions that need to be met and the considerations that need to be made for you to determine if shared parenting will work for you. I'm leaving out much of the background and context in this book as you can probably save the time at this point. You simply need to know what the arrangement is, how you can set it up and whether it is something that could work for you and your kids at this point in time.

The background and context included in the original book was worthy of inclusion in for a variety of reasons;

- It allowed the reader the chance to understand me, who I am and what my priorities in life are; I believe these facts in combination with the circumstances I found myself in were a big part of what had brought me to that point in life.

- It illustrated the context within which my shared-parenting arrangement with my ex-wife Jo had arisen and the critical success factors that have allowed it to flourish since.

This book has excluded much of the background since I appreciate that you are likely to have already decided that they are interested in implementing a shared-parenting structure in their lives for the benefit of their kids. Taking this assumption further, I envisage that you are newly divorced or at least on a path to divorce and sorting out the structure of parenting for your child is just one of the many matters of great significance that you need to resolve in the near future. As such, you are probably looking for a clear, structured and concise *manual* that will guide you rather than a *novel* from which you have to derive the practical steps. If you need further context or background, the original book is there for you to dip into. The first step is in deciding if it is for you and whether you can make it work.

Context and Definitions
I thought it would be useful to outline a few high level principles for the book to aid in clarity of understanding as you work your way through it.

I use 'divorce' as a general term for those who are divorced, separated or estranged from their partner. It is counter-productive to the intention of this book to do anything other than use these terms interchangeably. I believe that the advice and guidance within the book is equally applicable in all circumstances whether the divorced family comprises any number of children, whether of the same (or mixed) parentage, whether born to the couple or adopted. The couple may be heterosexual or same-sex. Fundamentally this book is concerned with catering to the needs of the children of a family within which the parents have decided to part but are interested in a non-conventional model of parenting.

If you decide to do further research on the topic (and I'd assume that since you've gone as far as picking up this book, you're planning on seeking further opinions), you may also see the terms shared-parenting and co-parenting used synonymously. From my perspective, whatever you call it, the structure amounts to much the same thing, or is at least driven from the same core principles.

To demonstrate these principles, I have outlined below a simplistic (perhaps over-simplified) definition of what I mean by shared-parenting by outlining a model of the structure. This can be used as the benchmark against which further suggestions and advice contained within this book are considered. It describes the model that has evolved for me and my ex over time, and represents that which I believe works best.

That isn't to say it's the *only* model that will work, but it can be used as the starting point from which you may be able to build your own arrangement.

- The children of the relationship spend their time 50% living with one parent and 50% with the other.

- The structure is based around a regular pattern of days (or weeks) when the kids move between each parent.

- Both parents live in reasonably close physical proximity during the weeks they have the kids. It may be that both parents retain a property for the weeks they have the kids, or that they both decide to remain based in the same general area, but the premise is that with either parent the child is able to attend the same school (or nursery, college, child-minder etc)

- Each parent strives to meet the financial costs of raising the child independently of support from the other. The divorce will presumably incorporate its own financial settlement anyway, based on either the ability of the parents to reach their own settlement as to the ongoing support that one parent will provide the other, or a court-decreed settlement. The intention is that each parent treats the fact that 50% of the time they have at least one extra mouth to feed, set of sports clubs to fund, and clothes and shoes to provide, as an accepted facet of their lives rather than a marginal cost for which they want to seek recompense from their ex.

- Each parent strives not to rely on the other parent to *any extent* during the weeks they have the kids. There may well be regular contact between the other parent and the kids, perhaps even a mid-week visit (subject to your agreement) but the key premise is that when you have the kids, they are yours to look after, provide for, pacify and cater to the whims of. You are parted from the other parent and should have no intention or expectation that they are there to support you when you have the kids any more than you will do the same when the kids are with them. This isn't a means for exerting a grudge, but rather to enforce that the parenting team isn't one of Mum and Dad together, but rather two separate parts of the same machine that work independently to achieve the same end goal.

- The set-up is structured, formal and repeatable in that both parents and the kids stick to a regular pattern, usually one week with one parent, the next week with the other, and so-on. The specific details such as whether the kids move between homes on a Monday, a Friday or whatever are somewhat irrelevant but the point is that it is structured and planned ahead and built into calendars. Aside from flexibility to juggle things around a bit at Christmas and to accommodate holidays, our schedule of calendars has been built into our diaries for at least the last 5 years without variation; one week on, one week off, switching on a Monday.

There are loads of other aspects to a shared parenting set-up, but those summarise what I believe we are striving for at a fundamental level

Is it for us?
Each and every aspect of shared-parenting should be informed by a number of core principles. I have summarised these below. I'm not overstating the value of these when I describe them as *Golden Rules* and at this stage and in the context of this book, you will have to take a leap of faith in believing that they have been derived

through years of experience. The background to the emergence of each of these rules is contained in my first book if you decide you are sufficiently interested to learn more, or want to challenge whether they are valid or not.

The rules are listed below for ease of reference. The remainder of the book will take each of the rules one by one and present you with:

- An overview of the key principles of the rule

- A number of things to consider in the application of the rules

- Where applicable, a series of quick questions you can ask yourself (and your ex-partner as they will need to be on-board with the proposed set up, or at least willing to contemplate it). It may be that these are prompts for discussion or that you actually want to write out answers to each and use this process to clarify your thinking. I'd suggest a mix of both in fact.

In working through these rules, each of which forms a chapter, I believe you will be able to arrive at a conclusion as to whether it is for you or not.

Just as the concept of shared-parenting is non-typical, I believe it's also advisable to treat the approach as something that you can pick and choose from to an extent. What I mean is that in practical terms you may not decide on a 50-50 split of parenting. This doesn't mean that you can't adopt shared-parenting principles into your separated family as a means of bettering all your lives. In this instance, the kids may not spend 50% of their time with each parent, but rather 70% with Mum and 30% with Dad, and so-on.

I contend that any model where the kids can spend more than alternate weekends and the odd-night here and there with Dad (or Mum) and where the parents can communicate, be seen to make decisions jointly, punish and reward the kids jointly and be seen to each want to play an active part in the kids' lives in spite of being divorced, is advantageous for the kids over a traditional separated model of parenting.

On this basis, I don't feel that the rules below should be treated as 'pass-or-fail' tests, or success criteria that you need to meet to make this work for you. Think of them instead of prompts that you should consider for the design of your future family-setup. Some of them are more essential than others, but see what you think.

Golden Rules in Summary

Golden Rule #1 – Each and every action, decision and guiding principle must be based around the needs of the kids and what is best for them.

Golden Rule #2 – The fundamental basis of the shared-parenting arrangement must be structured, repeatable, and enduring in its design to allow it to benefit the children (see Golden Rule #1) and to meet the needs of the parents

Golden Rule #3 – In combination with rigidity and structure, a shared-parenting arrangement must be able to flex as the needs of the child and the circumstances surrounding the arrangement (either short or long term) change.

Golden Rule #4 – Once Golden Rule #1 has been satisfied, it is okay for the shared-parenting arrangement to be designed for the mutual and individual benefit of the parents. Ensure though that it is equally beneficial otherwise resentments and negativity will creep in.

Golden Rule #5 – In agreeing the terms of a shared-parenting arrangement, there must be a consideration of the overall sustainability of the arrangement, and the effects it will have on the quality of life of the kids and the parents. If the terms of the arrangement require excessive compromise, expenditure, travel, or efforts to be made on a long-term basis then it is likely that the arrangement will at some point cease to work for everyone and may ultimately fail

Golden Rule #6 –The financial terms of a shared-parenting arrangement should always be negotiated, reviewed, managed and implemented separately from any other financial arrangements associated with the dissolution of the relationship. Treat any on-going payments that are not split equally between the parents as being focussed on the kids and maintain this distinction. Review the arrangement regularly and strive for an equitable 50/50 split

Golden Rule #7 –Once you have agreed to move forwards with the shared-parenting arrangement, establish it and immediately start living it (or do so as soon as it is realistically viable to). Apply the same approach to other key decisions, changes and in dealing with events that will doubtlessly occur and need to be managed throughout the arrangement. The time for action is always NOW.

Golden Rule #8 – It is advisable to think about a structured way of doing things, to help adapt to and maintain the shared-parenting arrangement, in as much or as little detail as you feel appropriate to yours and your kids' needs. Expect though that your structures and rules may be different from those of your ex, and don't feel pressured to adapt to their way of working. The key thing is that your overall goals, beliefs, aspirations and priorities for your kids are aligned which will ensure that your kids have a consistent parenting experience across both homes.

Golden Rule #9 – Whilst both parents are unlikely to agree on all matters that require a united-front of parenting, the key thing is to agree on the over-arching principles that shape your shared-parenting arrangement. Within this, matters such as expectations for the kids' behaviour, your aspirations and goals for them, the freedoms and disciplines you want them to grow-up with and the priorities for their upbringing should be understood and agreed upon by you both.

Golden Rule #10 – Where possible, agree on an approach to presenting a united front that ensures a level of trust and autonomy is given by Mum and Dad to each other to deal with the day-to-day in line with the overarching principles of the shared-parenting arrangement. In addition to this, ensure that you both agree with and understand the means by which you will handle the more serious or complex matters and ensure that you devote adequate time to this process.

Golden Rule #11 – Communication between you and your ex is CRITICAL to the successful maintenance of your shared-parenting. Ensure that you are able to discuss matters in a manner and with due consideration, time and sensitivity depending on the issue at hand.

Golden Rule #12 – Both of your children's places of residence should feel like and be treated as their homes. This sense should come about through both places being physically decorated to feel like home, with as few of their possessions following them about as possible to encourage a sense of permanence and belonging at both homes. A few basic principles can be adopted to ensure that the transit of 'things' between homes is kept to a minimum

Golden Rule #13 – It is imperative that you protect and preserve the sanctity and structure of your shared-parenting arrangement as you would protect your kids themselves. Do not allow yourself to be swayed by others be they friends, family, new partners or acquaintances in terms of being forced to modify any aspect unless it is specifically for the benefit of the children. In this case, such changes should be discussed and agreed with the person whom you share the parenting with.

Golden Rule #14 – As you enter into new relationships, and indeed as you contemplate any major life changes, ensure that you are being 100% true to yourself and ensuring that you don't waver on the things that are essential to you in living the life you want. Failing to do this will impact upon your happiness as a person, and on your ability to be the parent that you want to be to your kids.

Now that you hopefully understand the model of parenting that I am proposing, and the core rules that underpin it the rest of the book will assist you in deciding if you think it is something that will work for you.

Golden Rule #1

Each and every action, decision and guiding principle must be based around the needs of the kids and what is best for them.

The first of the Golden Rules cannot be over-emphasised in terms of its importance in dictating the overall success or failure that will emerge from entering into shared-parenting. If this isn't met, then there really isn't an arrangement to be made.

Key Principles of the Rule

On the face of it this rule is self-explanatory (most of them are!) however, I need to ensure that you appreciate the gravity of the rule and just how important it is.

The rule needs to be satisfied at the outset of setting up shared-parenting, but also within every stage, during every day of living with the arrangement thereafter. There is no decision or consideration from which exemptions can be granted from applying this rule.

Considerations when applying this rule are really limited to simply asking yourself whether the rule is being met or not. If the answer is yes, then you are likely to be on solid ground. If the answer is no then alarm bells should be ringing.

The fundamental basis is that if shared-parenting is based on anything other than it being the best and most practical means of meeting the multitude of needs that a child has from their parents, then it must be motivated by something else and is hence the arrangement will be likely to fail (either practically to fall apart or in the sense of failing in meeting the best interests of the parents and the kids). Such instances may include one or other parent entering into the arrangement out of a fear for losing contact if they don't (motivated by their own needs first and foremost), or a complacency since it's perceived as the easiest way of carving up the responsibility.

One parent may not wish to have the kids all the time, and hence might think they can package up their responsibility conveniently by sharing custody with their ex, but again this isn't necessarily motivated by what is best for the child.

A further, slightly abhorrent motivation (in my view) may be that one parent wishes to avoid making maintenance payments towards the upkeep of the kids and so figures that they'll take on custody of the kids 50% of the time. I dislike this view since it basically treats the kids as an expense item rather than focussing on their needs.

As long as each and every consideration regarding shared-parenting (including whether to enter into it in the first place) is shaped by the needs of the kids, and what is in their best interests, then you will be on solid ground.

Questions and considerations for the application of the rule

The following questions and prompts represent the considerations you and your ex need to make when contemplating shared-parenting. Some will be best considered by you individually, others by you together.

1. Am I capable (physically, mentally and emotionally) of being the sole-carer for my children for half the time?

   a. Can you honestly foresee yourself being able to fill all the roles that are required to raise a child, *on your own* for 50% of the time?

   b. Don't rule out that it is a learning curve and will most certainly require adaptation to you all. However, you should have a good gut-feel as to whether you believe you can do it or not. Determination is key.

2. Do you consider your ex to be capable (physically, mentally and emotionally) of being the sole-carer for my children for half the time?

   a. This isn't solely for you to judge since it may be that your emotions towards your ex are clouded at this time. There will undoubtedly be a shifting of roles, responsibilities and growing of capabilities that are needed as you set the structure up; both of you need to be able to adapt to this. The key question is whether you believe your ex to be capable to the extent that you can trust them to get on with it. If not, you will worry, meddle or try and influence their parenting which will erode the trust and structure within the setup. Bear in mind it also has be a mutual feeling from them too. If the matter is up for debate, then have the conversation and see if you can reach a consensus. It isn't a reason to start picking apart their character or parenting abilities but rather to surface all potential concerns on both sides and to see if you can agree whether the arrangement will work in principle.

3. Are there practical or legal reasons why shared-parenting must be ruled out?

   a. I am assuming that for the most part if the answer to this question was yes, then you wouldn't have bothered picking up the book in the first place. If one or other parent had a history of unmanaged mental illness, or had been violent towards your children (or you) or other serious and unthinkable abuse had been a feature in your lives then I am assuming that this is part of the reason why you are parting anyway. It would certainly not be in the best interests of the child to continue to be put in the way of danger.

   b. Practical reasons don't have to stem from a history of abuse or neglect. It may well be that one parent is significantly physically disabled or suffers from a chronic physical condition (such as epilepsy) and are hence unable to fulfil the parenting role on their own without support. For this reason, whilst both parents may be keen to retain an equitable share of the parenting responsibility, in practical terms it's unlikely to be feasible, at least at first. Nonetheless, you have good grounds to try and ensure that with appropriate support and adaptations both parents can maintain their input in the lives of the child.

   c. Further practical constraints may prevent a true shared-parenting arrangement from being established. If one parent has a job that demands ongoing mobility, travel and unsociable hours then those are going to present difficulties in meeting a structured and routine shared-parenting arrangement for their kids, even if both are keen to do so. This isn't to say that such jobs cannot be accommodated and maintained post-divorce alongside shared-parenting, and I have built a successful career as a freelance IT consultant regularly travelling around the country and Europe for work. However, the reality is that you are at a point in life where new family structures need as few challenges to them as possible. If you (or your ex) has a job where regular travel can be confined to the weeks when they don't have the children then this is less of a concern, but as with all considerations at this point you need to answer the question honestly to determine if it will be given a fighting chance from the off. If one or other of you is an airline pilot who is frequently away for days at a time, without a regular and repeating pattern of availability then this may be more of an issue.

4. Is this arrangement being pursued as a means of ensuring that you each pay-your-way towards the upbringing of the children?

   a. Considerations around splitting of financial responsibility for your kids (I'm not straying into the territory of all aspects of separating the finances of a failed relationship as it is far too large a topic) will be covered in other rules later in the book. Suffice to say at this point that one of the core principles is that shared-parenting is NOT intended to be the vehicle through which the finances of your relationship are resolved. I propose that you should strive to meet the costs associated with raising your children equally and each having them for 50% of the time and funding 50% of their costs is the desired end state. This question is intended to prompt you to consider whether you are considering shared-parenting out of fear that unless you share custody of the kids 50-50 your ex won't be receptive to sharing the costs of their upbringing. Such an arrangement would potentially gloss over a number of other negative factors (e.g. lasting resentment or potential for emotional blackmail between you) and wouldn't offer a solid and child-centric structure to be maintained. As such if the answer to this is yes, then I'd suggest you need to re-evaluate.

5. If your ex is already living with a new partner (or if adultery played a part in your split and there is likely to be a new person in the life of your ex), are you sufficiently comfortable with your kids seeing another person routinely when they are with your ex?

    a. This is complex and highly emotive, and even if this isn't a factor at the start of the shared-parenting arrangement, it undoubtedly will be at some point. The significance of it is greater at the outset though since in addition to going into a shared-parenting arrangement and having your kids for only half the time, it adds another complexity into the mix when there's a third party involved too. It's important that you are able to put any negative feelings aside or alternatively that you wait to set up shared-parenting at a later stage once wounds have healed a bit.

6. Are you going to be able to be an effective parent and meet all the diverse needs of your kids whilst on your own (accepting the learning curve that you and your ex will be on in the early days)?

    a. It will be challenging for you all to adapt to the change of circumstance in the short term, but do you feel realistically that you are committed to this, or are you doing it because you are fearful that you'll lose contact or value in the eyes of your kids (or in your own eyes)? Fear is a powerful motivator but not something that will guarantee you are doing the best you can for your kids or yourself, often in spite of your best intentions.

    b. Examples of this may include a mother needing to take up responsibilities regarding sports-coaching and handy-person for the kids where these were roles previously fulfilled by Dad. Similarly, with two teenage daughters I've had to step up when hormones and puberty have decided that the first purchase of sanitary towels naturally occurred when the girls were with me rather than their Mum. As a modern guy I was happy to rise to the challenge but there's no doubt that had the girls been raised in a traditional relationship then in this instance I would have directed them to their Mum.

7. Are your kids of a suitable age to be entering into a shared-parenting arrangement?

    a. The answer to this is never simple and age is not always a factor. One argument would be that a baby, not being breastfed (which would otherwise be a significant constraint on the viability of shared parenting) could be most adaptable to the prospect of shared-parenting (subject to both parents being sufficiently adaptable to care for a baby). In this instance, it is hard to imagine that the presence (or absence) of both parents has yet been a factor in the baby feeling loved and cared for (although there are undoubtedly scientific studies that will have investigated it). It might be an indicator that this is a perfect opportunity to undertake shared-parenting.

    b. An alternative and opposite view would be that such a child needs to be with its mother for the majority of time due to the formation and ongoing development of the 'mothering bond' in early years. It really all just depends on yours and your ex's views.

The above considerations touch upon a number of factors (but not all) that require consideration at the outset. Hopefully they prompt you to think about things in the context of what is best for the child first and foremost.

In even the most amicable divorces, there will be contention and discord between you and your ex. It can sometimes help both of you to put this aside and put yourself in the position of the child in order that a less emotive approach to decisions can be taken.

This first and most important golden rule should be treated as a subtext for all the others, so be sure you have this in mind throughout the rest of the book.

Golden Rule #2

The fundamental basis of the shared-parenting arrangement must be structured, repeatable, and enduring in its design to allow it to benefit the children (see Golden Rule #1) and to meet the needs of the parents

Key Principles of the Rule

When communications break down in the parting of a relationship and the separating couple is forced down the route of mediation or intervention from the legal system to work out the finer details of their split, a typical consequence is that the resulting set-up will be structured and rigid, to the point of being immovable. I'm pleased to say that this was never really contemplated in the parting of my marriage and I'm quite glad for that fact.

What is clear though is that such arrangements, whilst potentially lacking flexibility and the opportunity to incorporate reasonable give and take for each parent, that at least they let all the key participants in the arrangement know where they stand which is valuable for adults and kids alike.

The main sentiment behind this golden rule of shared-parenting then is to recognise the value of structure, clarity and predictability when it comes to working out the arrangements.

Regardless of how much any individual is able to 'go with the flow', I contend that we all like a degree of structure and routine in our lives, especially kids. In times of uncertainty we can often feel overwhelmed by the lack of structure surrounding the most fundamental aspects of life, and for kids (and their parents), especially in the aftermath of the separation of a family it's important that there is structure and repeatability in the basic aspects of the parenting arrangement. Things I'm including in this are as follows:

- How many nights the kids spend with each parent before switching between homes

- What night of the week they will switch on

20

- Whether they will have a regular phone or video-chat with the parent-B during their time with parent-A

- Where they stay when with each parent (it may be that each parent has their own home or when with one parent they are actually staying with extended family as well as the parent. Financial means may dictate that this is necessary in the first instance. The important factor is that it is structured and consistent from the outset)

- Whether they are in familiar surroundings and have belongings, clothes and pictures of their other parent and wider family around them. It must feel like being at home, not like visiting relatives.

The above list is not exhaustive, but illustrates the level that I'm thinking and which I'd encourage you to consider. Structure and rigidity does not mean that there can't be a degree of flexibility for all but the basic assumption is that for the most part everyone knows what the new normal will look like. The overlaying of flexibility as a secondary concern is important as it is a further valuable differentiator between shared-parenting and traditional models of parenting after divorce.

Questions and considerations for the application of the rule
The following questions and prompts illustrate the considerations you and your ex need to make when contemplating shared-parenting. Some will be best considered by you individually, others by you together.

1. Can you establish a living scenario where the kids are able to stay in the same general area (town, village, suburb etc) and attend the same school, nursery or college week-in, week-out?

   a. Consistency is important for kids, more than adults. Just because they are not necessarily of school-age or at an established nursery (for example) I'd contend it is important that they are not spending their time in two separate towns with two separate groups of people. This won't engender stability for them and is not a child-centric response to the circumstance (remember the golden rules are ALL compounded with Golden Rule Number 1!)

b. It may be that one parent remains in the former family home and the other takes up a new property or that you take up two new properties both of which are treated as home for the kids. To illustrate how far shared-parenting can be taken in progressive terms, as parents you may eventually come and go from the shared-parenting family home while the kids stay there full time and you obtain alternative accommodation elsewhere for when you aren't the parent of the week. This is perhaps the most revolutionary way of accommodating your separated family and is perhaps more of an aspiration too far when you're splitting. It took us 10 years before we took this step and it has given us all significant benefit since, but I can understand that at the outset it may not be the chosen means of housing. Whatever arrangement you arrive at the sentiment is that the kids know that whichever parent they are with, they are staying in a familiar place that is home to them.

2. Are you able to commit to a set pattern of parenting (e.g. 1 week on, 1 week off)?

a. The objective is to ensure that a repeatable pattern is preserved for all and that this is built into everyone's calendar for the foreseeable future. We have always done alternate weeks with the kids transitioning between us on a Sunday or Monday. This has meant that we finished our time with them on a notional 'high' in spending a weekend together after the rigours of a week had passed. This isn't the only way of accommodating things, but it has been easiest to manage and is treated as immovable by all involved.

b. At times, shaped by either mine or my ex's job we have flexed the arrangement to switch on a Sunday night to allow for work-related travel to alternative locations, but this was done in a structured rather than ad-hoc fashion.

3. Are you willing to manage work and social commitments on the basis of this schedule?

    a. There is no point in assuming that you can continue to live exactly as you have always done and to rely on the good will of others to mop up your childcare commitments, especially not your ex. Aside from the fact that you are parting and it would be unrealistic to expect them to be willing to be your on-call babysitter, it is potentially confusing and upsetting for your kids to still view you as co-dependent in this way.

    b. The key premise that I've always adopted is that when the kids are with me, I treat that as immovable (unless with exceptional justification) and plan all work travel, social occasions and other commitments in the time when I don't have the kids. If I do have a need for this to be changed, I will try and accommodate the requirement (e.g. a work meeting) within my schedule without having to call on my ex. This isn't out of bloody-mindedness but it signifies that I am striving to manage in a way that doesn't assume her co-operation or support, and equally she does the same. If I need to attend a social or work event in an evening when I have the kids, I enlist a babysitter who I pay rather than assuming my ex will have the kids for me. This isn't to say that we *never* do each other a favour or help each other out, but we don't assume each other's' support and they aren't the de-facto first point of call.

4. Can you manage your working schedule to the extent that shifts can be planned around your kids needing your time, or can this need be met via established child-care?

    a. In the full-length book I've included a chapter on work and managing your job around shared-parenting and you'll appreciate if you get to reading it that it is an area requiring significant focus. For the purposes of this exercise though, the key consideration is simply are you willing to make sure that your job is managed around your kids rather than vice-versa.

b. If you are a shift-worker, this will mean that you need to confine your unsociable hours around the weeks when you don't have your kids, and you will obviously need to surface this need with your employer early-on and up-front. In order to meet any other requirements for flexibility it's advisable to enlist the services of an accommodating child-minder (I'd recommend that both parents use the same one if possible, further enhancing the structure and predictability of the arrangement for the kids). This is what we did and over the years she and her family became like an extended part of ours.

c. If you have to work from a variety of locations, then it's necessary to become and expert at diary-management in order that work related travel is planned ahead for the weeks that you are kid-free. The same applies if you are regularly required to travel to meetings (e.g. a monthly divisional meeting in a location that isn't your usual place of work.) If you have a PA or some other individual who plans your travel, it is your responsibility to brief them fully on your circumstances and ensure this is factored into their planning of your diary.

5. Do you envisage being able to adapt your entire life towards having two separate patterns of life (with kids and without kids)?

a. If you foresee trouble adapting to this, it may well just be that you are going to require time to get used to the new normal (which is entirely understandable). However, your new reality will be that school holidays, family vacations, visits with your extended family, religious holidays, family events (e.g. weddings), family birthdays and so-on are all somewhat constrained or at least influenced by the additional consideration of your new parenting structures. It is important for your sanity and comfort that you are able to treat this as a fact of life rather than resisting, fighting or lamenting it.

b. My experience shows that family and friends are typically full of admiration for our parenting model, and often more than willing to accommodate my circumstances either to arrange events when I have, or don't have my kids depending on what is required.

6. Can you enlist the required support from within your family or network to make this arrangement work?

a. Historically I've been someone who struggles with asking others for help, mainly out of a sense of pride but also fierce independence. A reality of adapting to being a single-parent in any context, even within shared-parenting is that you will need help from time-to-time at least; we all do! The question is whether, with some forethought and planning you will be able to meet your commitments and afford your kids the normality that they deserve in life. For Dads in particular I suspect it's an unfamiliar role to be able to network with other parents to arrange play-dates, sleepovers and negotiate school pick-ups and drop-offs for your kids with help from other parents. Reality though is that is a normal part of raising kids (or so it seems to me) so there is no reason to resist this, or to miss out on you or your kids benefitting from such help.

b. You will need to accept that you can't do everything on your own, and any notional loss of pride you may fear through taking help will be more-than replaced by the pride you can take from doing the best for your kids.

Structure and rigidity are important factors for us all, in allowing us to feel comfort and security in our day-to-day lives. Ensure that these are built into your shared-parenting arrangement without losing sight of the need for flexibility occasionally, and you will have applied this golden rule successfully.

Golden Rule #3

In combination with rigidity and structure, a shared-parenting arrangement must be able to flex as the needs of the child and the circumstances surrounding the arrangement (either short or long term) change.

Key Principles of the Rule

The similarity between shared-parenting and a family whose separation has been overseen by the courts is in the structure and rigidity that both arrangements incorporate. A significant difference however is that there is an implicit understanding (borne out of the principle of Golden Rule number 1) that the parents are co-operative, communicative and willing and able to demonstrate flexibility around the arrangement from time-to-time in order to make things easier than they might otherwise be.

I'm not thinking in this instance of being on-call babysitters for each other (see the previous chapter) or of there being constant liberties taken in relation to covering each other's commitments. Examples of the flexibility I consider reasonable will be:

- Facilitating the kids going to an event in the family of your ex (e.g. a wedding) when it falls within your week, by allowing some flexibility and diversion from your schedule; the child will benefit from being part of rather than excluded from a family event

- Covering a school parents evening when it doesn't fall within your week, both as your ex can't make it but as you also want to attend and present a united front as well as taking an interest in the progress of your child at school

- Allowing the shifting of weeks around a bit so that your ex can take the kids on a 2 week holiday; the child will presumably enjoy a holiday

- Taking a couple of days off to have the kids during a school holiday when it falls in a week the kids are due to be with your ex. This demonstrates that your role as parent pervades through all time, even when they're not scheduled to be with you.

Questions and considerations for the application of the rule

The following questions and prompts illustrate the considerations you and your ex need to make when contemplating shared-parenting. Some will be best considered by you individually, others by you together.

1. Do you consider yourself to be free of resentments towards your ex such that you can generally consider reasonable requests for assistance in the context of whether it has a positive impact for your kids?

    a. The consideration of the impact for the kids should always be what drives the request for assistance, and the response to the request. This criterion should mean that no genuinely reasonable requests get made or turned down.

    b. The above represents an ideal-world view, and isn't always going to be realistic in the context of your relationship having parted. However, the general premise should always be that *in spite of your differences* if you can consider requests for help in the context of the benefit to your kids then you will be doing your best to service the arrangement.

2. Are you able to accommodate change in terms of being able to flex to meet the needs of your kids, within the bounds of what you can reasonably accommodate?

    a. The need here is to ensure that the fundamental needs of the kids are best met by you and your ex, and to reflect that sometimes there will be a need to make changes to arrangements based on the needs of the kids.

    b. As your kids reach their teenage years for example, you may find that the rigid structure is no longer the best means of meeting the kids needs and instead you need to flex rather than pushing them back and forth between homes as the calendar dictates. Younger kids however may also at times have a genuine need to not rigorously conform to the normal schedule based on a need to be with one parent or the other. Can you adapt to this?

c. A birthday party of a close friend or cousin on your side of the family may fall in the week they are with your ex; can you foresee being able to make reasonable changes to the schedule to allow their attendance at this?

3. Can you reasonably accept and delegate responsibilities between you and your ex and accept that these responsibilities may at certain points in the upbringing of your kids, change?

a. As with a successful relationship, there has to be a delegation of roles and responsibilities between parents and the same remains true within a shared-parenting arrangement. For example, I've always been responsible for taking the kids to dentists and doctors' appointments and eye-tests etc. However, as time has gone by the girls have become more comfortable with their Mum accompanying them to the doctors and so we've sought to balance things out a bit more. The flexibility here is that over time the arrangement and its terms and conditions may change and flex; things don't necessarily stay the way they've always been during the shared-parenting arrangement (which is for the long term) any more than they did when you split up.

b. As the kids get older and their interests more diverse we've gone through numerous phases of delegating between us the role of 'parent in attendance' at things such as sporting competitions, musical performances and school plays and assemblies. This isn't something of great complexity to manage and I'm keen not to overplay the importance of this, but the fact is that we do have to be flexible and accept that as time passes and the kids get older there will be more diverse roles that needs to be fulfilled and flexibility in who fills these needs to be accepted as part of the demands of shared-parenting.

Flexibility is required at all levels at times; it may at points be necessary to make changes to fundamental elements of the structure around your shared-parenting and at other times, minor tweaks get made. In making these changes you make a strong statement to the outside world but more importantly to your kids and to you and your ex that you are able to adapt, flex and evolve. A pattern that is fixed and immovable for the long-term will inevitably suffer eventually, causing harm for all those in it.

Golden Rule #4

Once Golden Rule #1 has been satisfied, it is okay for the shared-parenting arrangement to be designed for the mutual and individual benefit of the parents. Ensure though that it is equally beneficial otherwise resentments and negativity will creep in.

Key Principles of the Rule

A fundamental lesson that I learned somewhat later in life than I would have liked is the realization that a happy me makes for a happy me in all spheres of my life, whether as a father, employee, friend, partner, son or any other capacity. One of the many beauties of shared-parenting (if it is something that is truly for you and can be adapted to successfully by your separated family) is that it not only benefits your kids, but also you and your ex. The key point for the purposes of this golden rule is that you should be 100% okay with that fact and embrace it, not resist it or feel guilty for it.

Once you have got to grips with the arrangement and you, your ex and most importantly your kids are settled into it you will start to see the numerous benefits for yourself. The kids get equal (or approaching-equal) input from both parents in their lives rather than the sporadic involvement of one parent that is more typical in separated families. The kids get two sets of input to their upbringing, greater involvement from the wider extended-families, more continuity with their former lives and potentially less of a sense of loss of any one parent. As the ethos from both parents will be aligned (a core requirement) it is also way less confusing for the kids at a younger age, and as such any potential backlash that you may face is lessened.

For the parents as individuals there are obvious and immediate benefits too. Where one parent in a typical separated family might otherwise be responsible for the kids for around 18 days (and nights) per month, instead with a more equitable split they are able to recharge and recuperate on a regular basis, and to have more time to themselves for their own benefit, growth and social lives. I won't deny that there is still the tendency to miss the kids when they're away from me and I know the same is and has always been true for their Mum. However, the reality is that once you can get a guilt-free appreciation of this time and see it for the many beneficial effects it has, the better the arrangement will serve all involved.

The other key aspect of the rule is the need for both parents to benefit equally from it to avoid resentment on anyone's part.

The nub of this matter is that in protecting the arrangement, you should be able to maintain a respectful distance from your ex and the sanctity of the arrangement should be preserved meaning that both parents have an equal opportunity to enjoy their kids-free time. When this doesn't happen, there can be a danger that parent A sees parent B as exploiting their involvement as a glorified-babysitter or some other misconstrued view of the situation and this can then undermine the set-up. Managed badly this can erode the very fabric of the set-up, but done well it is a massive benefit.

In simple terms, if you can ensure that you each feel the benefit of the arrangement then you should both do so, and feel no guilt about doing so. You will be a better parent to your kids as a result of this, and that will benefit everyone.

Questions and considerations for the application of the rule

The following questions and prompts illustrate the considerations you and your ex need to make when contemplating shared-parenting. Some will be best considered by you individually, others by you together.

1. Will you be able to accept that when the kids are with you that your ex will be moving on with their life, pursuing their social life, taking advantage of their free-time and rebuilding their lives?

   a. This is essential to accept, and if it links to a wider dissatisfaction or lack of acceptance of your ex moving on, then it may be that the time is not right overall for entering into shared-parenting.

   b. This should really be something that is treated as sub-conscious and baked-in to the arrangement rather than being something you actively think about. When the kids are with you, your focus should be upon them, not wondering or being in any way aware of what your ex is doing with their time. When the kids are with them, you don't cease to be interested in the kids or wonder what they are up to, but this is your time to focus on the other aspects of your life that slip down the priority list when you have the kids.

2. Will you be able to get on with your own life and make the best of your kids-free time?

   a. You may use this as an opportunity to pursue any number of hobbies or pastimes or simply to catch up on rest, work or social engagements that have been missed out on due to commitments with your kids when they were with you.

   b. The fact of the situation is that this is how the balance of your life will be preserved and so it's up to you to ensure you make the best of this situation and embrace it as your reality.

3. Can you envisage being able to make the most of your time, free of guilt that you should be spending more time and mental energy on your kids?

   a. The reality is that in entering shared-parenting you are doing an amazing thing and putting your kids first in your life. There is nothing to feel guilty about, and if it takes you time to learn and appreciate this fact, then put your trust in that fact and allow time to prove it.

   b. If you suffer particularly regarding guilt, there is an extensive chapter within the full book covering off this topic, my thoughts on it, and how I have learned to manage and eradicate feelings of guilt over the years.

In my experience there have been numerous benefits that I have experienced personally, which I attribute largely to the shared-parenting structure we have in place and which has shaped other aspects of my life. Factors as pivotal as the opportunities I've received and taken in my work, the growth of myself as a person and even the subsequent relationship with my second wife have all been made possible and even brought forwards as a result of the shared-parenting arrangement I have in place.

I'd suggest that equal benefits can be reasonably expected by others in a similar circumstance if you are willing to adopt and embrace shared-parenting and establish it in the right way and for the proper reasons.

Golden Rule #5

In agreeing the terms of a shared-parenting arrangement, there must be a consideration of the overall sustainability of the arrangement, and the effects it will have on the quality of life of the kids and the parents. If the terms of the arrangement require excessive compromise, expenditure, travel, or efforts to be made on a long-term basis then it is likely that the arrangement will at some point cease to work for everyone and may ultimately fail

Key Principles of the Rule

Whilst this book, and my experiences upon which it is based clearly advocate shared-parenting as the best way of parenting your kids post-divorce, like any long term arrangement or choice we make in life it has to be established on solid footings if it has a chance of succeeding in the long-term.

I've known many others who've admirably done their best to establish an effective separated family structure in the circumstances within which they lived post-divorce, ranging from the conventional (typical court-decreed set-up) through to an example where the two parents lived in London and Paris and the father used to fetch his daughter on the Eurostar once or twice per month.

Any set-up can be made to work *in theory* but the chances of enduring success will be hindered if the terms, conditions and parameters are too much of a stretch for any one party.

An excessive cost (which can be a side effect of maintaining multiple homes or the travel costs associated with keeping the kids in the same schools and holding down jobs) can be an immediate challenge to the set-up. Similarly, if one parent is clearly not going to compromise on where the arrangement is established and is looking to cling on to all the parts of your former relationship that they liked, but without sharing it with you then this too will present an inherent challenge from the outset.

The fundamental aim in this instance is that if you think that shared-parenting will be a possible solution for your family post-divorce, then step-two is to look at the high level practicalities that would likely be involved and consider if these are realistic and achievable. They may not initially be feasible as things stand for you and your ex, but with a carefully considered plan you can adapt to make it possible (assuming all other conditions are met). Fundamentally though, there is no point in considering or enacting radical plans for change if the resulting situation is going to be so challenging or tenuous as to give it no ongoing chance of lasting.

Questions and considerations for the application of the rule

The following questions and prompts illustrate the considerations you and your ex need to make when contemplating shared-parenting. Some will be best considered by you individually, others by you together.

1) Do you foresee the associated costs that will be required to service two homes for you and your kids as being achievable from your existing incomes?

    a. Management of the finances of shared-parenting has its own golden rule, but in this context the overall question is regarding the viability of whether the costs can be met at a high level to maintain two homes for the kids. This means that the costs can be met without radical additional income being sought (e.g. a second night-job) or excessive cost-cutting on the part of one or other parent that won't be sustainable.

    b. Costs can be managed, and shared-parenting doesn't necessarily mean two lots of rent or mortgage repayments plus bills for two homes; it may be that initially the kids may have one home with parent-A in the house that was formerly the family home, and when they are with parent-B they stay in a devoted space with wider family (e.g. at the home of their grandparents). The key thing that's requierd to engender some ongoing sense of permanence and structure is that the kids need two defined places for their time with each parent so that it's not the case of being transient or nomadic when they're with one or other parent.

2) Will the logistical arrangements be achievable for you and your ex in the context of a shared-parenting structure?

   a. Excessive travel (for example if you live away in a distant place in the weeks when you don't have the kids) can be managed depending on your own resilience but will place challenges on you in terms of travel time and expenditure. I have had prolonged spells of a few months at a time working away in London during the weeks when I wasn't living in Manchester with the girls, and this was very manageable but I did get used to living out of a suitcase more than usual! It can be done, but needs to be planned for and managed. In this instance, the work-related travel gets built into your schedule (as previously mentioned) and you accept that you need to be more organised to ensure that you have the things you need with you, wherever you are. It can be sustainable, but as with all things you will know what this means for you individually.

3) Can yours and your ex's work commitments be accommodated with due consideration of childcare, or will shared-parenting effectively serve to put either of your livelihoods at risk?

   a. This isn't a means of saying that work comes first, but practically speaking we all need an income, particularly if we're functioning to support kids as well as ourselves!

   b. If you foresee that it's simply not practical to maintain your livelihoods as a result of you both fulfilling the parenting role for 50% of the time then this may prevent shared-parenting. However, the demands of time and cost could vary enormously depending on the age of your kids (who may not need you at home anywhere near as long if they're in full-time schooling).

   c. Fundamentally, you cannot conceive of entering into shared-parenting 50/50if in the long-term it will threaten your ability to hold down your job and you are the primary breadwinner for your separated family.

This doesn't have to mean though that shared-parenting is rejected out of hand, but rather that you and your ex consider an arrangement that reflects the various constraints upon it.

There are numerous factors that might make a situation sustainable or not. As with most aspects of life though, you have the freedom of choice from the outset to design your shared-parenting arrangement from the ground-up. Its sustainability is of great importance, particularly considering the knock-on effects it will have for your child if the arrangement itself falls apart when they've potentially just got used to it following your divorce.

Sustainability also equates to a reduction in pressure and stress that the arrangement has potential to exert on you and your ex. If the set-up is testing to the point of frailty then you'll both be fighting to make it work, and I can assure you that as with any aspect of parenting, traditional or non-traditional we need fewer challenges, not more!

Golden Rule #6

The financial terms of a shared-parenting arrangement should always be negotiated, reviewed, managed and implemented separately from any other financial arrangements associated with the dissolution of the relationship. Treat any on-going payments that are not split equally between the parents as being focussed on the kids and maintain this distinction. Review the arrangement regularly and strive for an equitable 50/50 split

Key Principles of the Rule

Financial settlements in divorce can be amongst the most contentious parts of any split and can surpass the emotional pain for some! The implication if you are considering shared-parenting is that you're already someway ahead of others in the emotional maturity stakes and can see that splitting up isn't a means of scoring points off the other, or securing custody of your kids as a means of punishing your ex. However it's almost unavoidable that there won't be at least some sort of financial settlement that is required to allow the set-up to work.

My contention here is that if you can separate the finances associated with raising your kids from wider finances (e.g. the splitting assets and apportioning debt) then this will serve you all well. It's not a case of putting a cost on the day-to-day running costs of your kids but if you can strive for the situation where, if only conceptually, that you are financially responsible for the kids when they are living with you then this will be a good start in separating the kids from the money.

The overall situation may well be the parent A provides a set monthly payment to parent B to level out incomes in respect of differing professions that each has, but this should be put aside as a factor in whether the kids spend their time with one parent or the other. If, over time, (as has been the case since my divorcing) a position of greater equity is reached between what the parents each earn then such financial subsidies may cease. At this point you are then effectively sharing all aspects of parenting including meeting the financial costs as well as the responsibility and time commitment.

Questions and considerations for the application of the rule

The following questions and prompts illustrate the considerations you and your ex
need to make when contemplating shared-parenting. Some will be best considered
by you individually, others by you together.

1) Golden rule number 5 touched upon the high level issue of costs. To revisit
   this with more substance, can you foresee that between you and your ex that
   you can meet the costs of:

   a. Two homes (and associated bills) if you choose to go down the route
      of providing two separate homes. Alternative options include

      i. One parent maintaining a home for them and the kids when
         they have them, the other parent living with wider family and
         the kids being allocated a devoted space within that home – this
         is of course reliant on the long-term good-will of family

      ii. A single property being provided for the kids, and a room being
          equipped as something of a hotel-room for the parent of the
          week – We have moved to this model in the last year, and it
          works brilliantly for the kids in not having to move about, and
          for us in terms of saving money. It does however require good
          management of boundaries between you, division of
          responsibility and openness about management of money to
          name three key challenges. It could work for all involved, but I
          speculate it may be best suited to older kids, or at least used as
          a long-term solution once the divorce has been completed, all
          are used to the situation and any lasting acrimony and
          resentment has been dealt with.

   b. Multiple sets of clothing (within reason – there's no need to buy two
      sets of everything, but over time it might make sense to limit the
      amount of clothes and toys etc that transit between the two homes)

      i. We have found over time that it makes sense to have a couple of sets of casual clothing and shoes (trainers for example) but you need half as much at each property since they can only wear it half as much. Similarly, it's good to have chargers for gadgets at each home since always seem to get lost in transit. Beyond that, they only need one set of school uniform and a few toys at each location and you're more or less equipped.

    c. Food and Childcare (this doesn't double up, but should be the same as was the case for you pre-split, albeit that you each meet half the costs)

2) Can you notionally separate any financial support you may be providing to your ex (e.g. to reapportion equity from a former marital home, or to apportion debt from the marriage) as part of your divorce, from any financial support you are providing to enable shared-parenting?

    a. The difference in my experience is that it is easier to accept that any high-level reapportionment of money or debt as part of the divorce is dealt with as a matter of law, duty or honour that is entirely separate from any financial support that I provided in the past for my kids. This means that any resentment or acrimony can be dealt with as part of a process that is entirely separate from the kids.

    b. When I split from my ex, there were financial terms of the divorce relating to property and assets, but separate to this we agreed that I would pay a sum of £300 per month to her to reflect that we aspired to share parenting of the kids and at the point we started this arrangement I earned £40k per year and she earned £20k. With this assistance we could both meet the core costs of their upbringing, notionally separately without having to frequently reapportion costs as they came up or review every expenditure in detail. I viewed this as me paying £300 per month towards food and clothing for the kids when they were with their Mum rather than me topping up her income by £300 and feeling cheated when she had a night out and spent this on beer. It's a subtle distinction, but I believe it's essential if only for your own personal sanity to keep the arrangement working.

c. When additional expenditures come up (e.g. school trips or the need for unusual items of clothing (e.g. winter coats, school shoes etc) then you can negotiate these separately to the wider arrangement. In our instance, we have found that one-off costs like school trips are split between us either equally or closer to equally. Items such as school shoes we take in turn to purchase for each child. These costs are then managed effectively and openly without being allowed to fester and become points of resentment later down the line.

Few subjects have the potential to be as emotive or cause as much argument as money in even the most healthy of relationships. In shared-parenting, between a divorced couple this could have even more potential for causing upset if not managed effectively.

As such, it's important to give this significant open discussion from the outset, and to try and maintain open and honest communication throughout (more on this later).

Make sure to separate the financial terms of parenting from the wider financial settlements from your divorce to ensure that your emotions don't compromise your ability to parent your kids together as you wish to.

Golden Rule #7

Once you have agreed to move forwards with the shared-parenting arrangement, establish it and immediately start living it (or do so as soon as it is realistically viable to). Apply the same approach to other key decisions, changes and in dealing with events that will doubtlessly occur and need to be managed throughout the arrangement. The time for action is always NOW.

Key Principles of the Rule

This isn't so much an ongoing rule but a decision point as far as you are concerned right now; considering whether shared-parenting is for you or not. In all but a handful of specific circumstances (e.g. if your kids are perhaps so young as to need to be primarily with their mum due to being breast-fed) then I contend that the only time to do this is now. Right now. Just like the very act of having kids, there really isn't a best time to enter into shared-parenting. The only way you can really determine if it will suit you all is to determine it is viable and to then dive in headlong, to give it a go, be adaptable and consider all the other golden-rules as you go along.

If you find that it works for you, and subsequently get settled into a routine with it you will see that it was the right thing for you all. That doesn't mean that there won't on occasion be times when you need to amend the setup, make changes to the way you do certain things, or adapt to changes in circumstances of one or more of the relevant parties (e.g. you change your job or the kids move schools). You may even at times question if it was the right thing to do altogether (although I can assure you that in most cases you are just experiencing natural doubts and challenges that all parents experience). When these forces for change come about and you have to decide on amendments to the set-up, once again the only time that you should take action is now, not at some point in the future once you've procrastinated over it a little longer.

Questions and considerations for the application of the rule

The following questions and prompts illustrate the considerations you and your ex need to make when contemplating shared-parenting. Some will be best considered by you individually, others by you together.

1) Do you genuinely believe that shared-parenting represents the best means of raising your kids between you and your ex?

2) Can you see a way that the high level challenges of shared-parenting (e.g. costs, logistics, variation and distribution of roles and responsibilities between you and your ex) can be met?

3) Are you and your ex equally convinced of the potential benefits and equally committed to taking this on?

4) Are you comfortable that those around you whose views and input you value, understand and appreciate why you are doing this?

If you can answer a resounding (or almost resounding) 'YES' to all these questions, then I'd contend you are in a good place to go-ahead and get shared-parenting in place NOW!

The subject of objectors to shared-parenting, and how to treat the views of others is touched upon in this book and dealt with at length in the full version of the book. However, if you are someone who places great value on the opinion of close friends and family and are keen not to ignore the wise-counsel of those who know you best, I strongly recommend getting them to read either this book or the full one and to discuss your intentions with them at length. In my experience, it's good to have the courage of your convictions but it is also wise to feel like you've thoroughly explored all well-meaning advice offered to you, even if you subsequently choose to ignore it.

The time for action in regard to shared-parenting is NOW, but that shouldn't be confused with being a driver to act with haste and to take decisions that you later regret.

Golden Rule #8

It is advisable to think about a structured way of doing things, to help adapt to and maintain the shared-parenting arrangement, in as much or as little detail as you feel appropriate to yours and your kids' needs. Expect though that your structures and rules may be different from those of your ex, and don't feel pressured to adapt to their way of working. The key thing is that your overall goals, beliefs, aspirations and priorities for your kids are aligned which will ensure that your kids have a consistent parenting experience across both homes.

Key Principles of the Rule

If you are ever of a mind to read the full story or my shared-parenting of my kids then you'll learn in depth of the challenges that I, a meticulously organized, military-style parent have had in accepting the more laissez-faire approach favoured by my ex, the girls' mother.

When setting up my side of the shared-parenting arrangement, preparing for when my girls were with me, I found that the best possible way that I could work the situation was to plan meticulously, be as organised as I could be and to implement structured methods and schedules to ensure that we all got through the day. I saw this as *the* way to do things and couldn't see beyond the timetables and plans that meant that we got through each day successfully relatively happy and unscathed.

I would overhear comments from the girls that suggested that things were far more free-form at their Mums' house and couldn't see how this could possibly work, or more importantly how the girls didn't find this all very confusing. The conclusion that I reached though after a great deal of consideration was that the practicalities of the arrangement didn't matter so much as the underlying goals, beliefs, priorities and values behind the parenting of both me and their Mum. We both valued the same core things, we prioritised the importance of their happiness, contentedness, wellbeing, sense of being loved and the value of good behaviour, respect for others and working hard at school. Factors such as expectations over whether they got changed out of school uniforms with 10 minutes of getting in from school, when dinner was served, when homework was done, or who chose what to watch on TV were frankly insignificant. The important factor was that all the good things and important things were catered for and taken care of, and underpinned by a core set of beliefs that were the same in both homes.

The important thing in life in this context is to ensure that yours and the kids' lives are sufficiently structured when they are with you to meet the practicalities of the day-to-day life and to allow you all to function happily. If you (like me) are a born-organiser, the apply this skill to the aspects of the day that you find potentially daunting or stressful. If your ex is different to you, accept that they will do things their way. Most important is that you and your ex continue to embrace the same core parenting values and that these are apparent to your kids in both homes.

Questions and considerations for the application of the rule

The following questions and prompts illustrate the considerations you and your ex need to make when contemplating shared-parenting. Some will be best considered by you individually, others by you together.

1) Do you feel confident that with some foresight and planning you can take on all the challenges that you can foresee in parenting the kids when they are with you?

    a. You may draw up lists, schedules, timetables and plans for who does what and when. Your ex may just let things happen and correct and guide the kids when they stray off course; either way, if the same outcomes are delivered it is entirely down to the individual

2) Can you adapt to the various roles that shared-parenting will demand of you?

    a. There are numerous roles ranging from cook, nurse, handy-man, sports coach, chauffeur, cleaner, entertainer and teacher (as well as many more) and each of these needs to be adopted by both parents to some extent at least. Ensure that you equip yourself accordingly to deliver each of these so that the kids have a consistent experience between both homes.

3) Are you flexible and capable when it comes to dealing with the challenges that parenting will throw up from time-to-time and of mostly dealing with these on your own?

    a. I'm fairly confident that even if you think the answer to this is 'No', the answer is probably 'Yes' to the same degree that *any* parent could answer 'Yes'. Parenting is such a challenge that I doubt anyone really can say 'Yes' all the time! You are clearly a resourceful and smart person for even contemplating a different way of doing things, and this resourcefulness will serve you well.

4) Can you accept that whilst you might have one way of doing the most simple of things as regards your kids (e.g. what time they go to bed when they're with you, or whether you eat meals at the dining table) that your ex might have a completely different way of doing things?

    a. If you genuinely believe that the underlying ethos is the same with both parents, then such details shouldn't matter as much as it may annoy you or you may be convinced that your way is the best, and one-and-only way!

    b. It will only serve to annoy you and potentially strain relations between you and your ex if you strive to make them do things the way you do; indeed this inherent difference in the way you do things may be part of why you split up! Consider that the kids happiness in either home is in part (a significant part at that) influenced by the happiness of the parent they are with. If you are doing things your way, you'll be happier and this will be felt by the kids. The same goes for when they're with their other parent.

5) Are you and your ex clear on the values, behaviours and beliefs that should underpin the parenting ethos in both homes?

a. This will doubtless require a little discussion but I'm thinking of topics such as respect for others, manners, diligence regarding schoolwork, time allowed for watching TV/playing computer games, behavioural expectations, curfews, allowances, chores they should do, manners and so-on. Most of these should be easily identified but should also be explicitly agreed or understood between you both (and shouldn't be difficult to agree on).

b. When these are known, you can then enjoy the fact that in spite of practical differences in your approaches, the ethos in each home is the same.

This golden rule is as much about the parent as the child and you as an individual. It is essential that you are as happy as possible in day to day life both for your own benefit as much as for the kids. If lingering frustrations or resentment regarding your ex are likely to diminish this and you're already contemplating a position where you are going to remain closer to your ex than you might traditionally be post-divorce. As such, this rule is about adopting a healthy mind-set that allows you to function in ways that bring you comfort but also which affords them the same courtesy.

The net-effect of this is likely to be reduced tension, greater acceptance and more happiness for all involved.

Golden Rule #9

Whilst both parents are unlikely to agree on all matters that require a united-front of parenting, the key thing is to agree on the over-arching principles that shape your shared-parenting arrangement. Within this, matters such as expectations for the kids' behaviour, your aspirations and goals for them, the freedoms and disciplines you want them to grow-up with and the priorities for their upbringing should be understood and agreed upon by you both.

Key Principles of the Rule

This rule follows on closely from the previous one. In simple terms, this is about making sure that you don't create a situation where either you, your ex or the kids view the shared-parenting structure as a means of exerting influence over others, of acting deceitfully, or of excusing bad behaviour. Once you've set out your core values and shared principles that will apply consistently in both homes, there may on occasion be a need for these to be enforced (by punishment or reward). There needs to be some clarity of understanding that in such instances where this becomes necessary, there will be consistency in its application between homes.

The underlying premise of this book is that you and your ex have parted or are in the process of parting, whether to separate or divorce. I further assume that this was for one or a number of reasons that all boil down to you and your ex not getting on in one way or another. You've split up, and with the commitment to jointly raising your kids you're going to have to remain closer than many might feel comfortable in remaining with their ex on a regular basis. This will also retain close and regular exposure to their views and actions and you will of course be required to manage your reactions to this.

What you have committed to doing more of (than just 'getting through') is to retain joint commitment to values, priorities and beliefs as regards our parenting of your children. It is in the application of rules to enforce this (amongst many other things) that you must remain united and communicative.

Questions and considerations for the application of the rule

The following questions and prompts illustrate the considerations you and your ex need to make when contemplating shared-parenting. Some will be best considered by you individually, others by you together.

1) Do you have trust in your ex that they will apply the same rules, discipline and expectations of behaviour that you both wish to be used in the upbringing of your kids?

   a. This will in essence be the practical translation of many of your core values defined under Golden Rule #9. In many instances the enforcement of these will come down to simple rules (e.g. bedtime at 8pm to enable 10 hours sleep on a school night) but in other cases it may be more involved. Two parents, one of whom is vegetarian and the other isn't (for example) but who decide to raise their kids as vegetarian may find that the non-vegetarian struggles to resist the child's demands to share their bacon! This is quite a trite example, but it illustrates my point that if something is defined as a core value, both parents must trust each other to enforce and apply rules that preserve and support it.

2) Do you understand what expectations your ex has of you in this regard and do you believe you will be able to apply this?

   a. The arrangements in this instance (and all others) need to be reciprocal between you and your ex. You may have residual issues of trust towards your ex stemming from the parting of your relationship, but it is essential to understand and align to their expectations regarding the kids, and for them to do the same.

3) Can you foresee any instances where your kids may consider exploiting the arrangement for their own benefit or to act deceitfully?

   a. This sounds more serious than it should perhaps, but the key point here is that if you think your kids could have scope to exploit the divisions between you then there could be significant challenges from the off. This is of course more likely for older kids or teenagers than younger kids but you will know and understand the motivations of your kids and how well the arrangement is likely to work for them. Examples may include:

i.   Telling parent A that parent B allows them to watch late night television if they can't sleep

ii. Telling parent A that they are staying at the home of parent B when in reality they're going to a party at a friends house

The above examples demonstrate scenarios that could arise in any non-separated family as well, and the prospect of these shouldn't be barriers to shared-parenting, but rather are things that you need to give some thought to from the outset. In plain terms, it's about trusting your ex to apply your rules and expectations and being honourable in doing the same for them. If punishments (or rewards) are set out when they are with your ex, and they should span time with the kids are due to be with you as well, respect that and don't seek to be the 'good guy' by neglecting this commitment. It is the willingness to adopt these roles and responsibilities that is of such importance as far as shared-parenting is concerned.

Golden Rule #10

Where possible, agree on an approach to presenting a united front that ensures a level of trust and autonomy is given by Mum and Dad to each other to deal with the day-to-day in line with the overarching principles of the shared-parenting arrangement. In addition to this, ensure that you both agree with and understand the means by which you will handle the more serious or complex matters and ensure that you devote adequate time to this process.

Key Principles of the Rule

Again, this rule follows on from the previous one. Undoubtedly, you'll be keen to avoid from the off, the tendency that kids can have to want to play one parent off against the other. This is no doubt a factor in any relationship or non-separated family, and was certainly a ploy I used as a kid. Once you're established in a shared-parenting structure, you'd be right to anticipate that the kids have all the more scope to exploit this, telling one parent they're at the other parent's house whilst actually being at another place entirely.

The principle behind this golden rule is to establish the culture where to the kids minds, both parents are equally empowered to make rules, enforce punishments and make expectations of behaviour that represent them jointly. This equally applies to decisions that need to be taken on a day-by-day, week-by-week basis. Both parents should have the right (empowered by the other) to make decisions that will then be followed-through by the other parent.

In an age where everyone is only a text, instant message or telephone call away, it's all too easy for kids to seek for one parent to interject on their behalf, almost in real-time. I'm suggesting here that in separated families (and in families in general for that matter) that one parent's word should be law, just as much as the other should be. An outer veil of unity is an absolute necessity, and I'd hope this isn't even a veil but more an accurate reflection of the truth.

There will also be matters that require more serious consideration or conversation so it's also imperative that you and your ex are receptive to regular communication to discuss topics that require a combined and considered response.

Questions and considerations for the application of the rule

The following questions and prompts illustrate the considerations you and your ex need to make when contemplating shared-parenting. Some will be best considered by you individually, others by you together.

1) Do you trust your ex to apply rules, punishments and expectations of behaviour that you both agree on?

2) Are you willing to entrust your ex to apply punishments that you have implemented?

   a. You may decide to ban your kids from watching TV for two weeks for a particular misdemeanour. If your ex isn't willing to implement this punishment, or if you think they'll take pity on the child and crumble in the face of nagging, then this may indicate that you either can't trust them to act in accordance with your views. Alternatively you may need to amend your views of whether punishments can span beyond the times the kids are with you.

3) Are you willing to enforce the punishments that your ex may implement?

4) Are you willing and able to devise joint motivational schemes or incentives that can be offered to your kids jointly?

   a. It's not just in punishments that you need to be unified. If you both value the importance of school work, you may wish to offer a financial incentive or a treat for your child if they achieve certain grades or a score in an examination. In my view and experience, it would be good for this to be offered jointly as equal parents (and funded jointly too)! If you don't wish to do this jointly, it would still be good if your approach could be aligned so that you both offer a reward for a certain achievement (and preferably that neither incentive eclipses the other).

5) Are you willing to entrust your ex to make decisions on a regular basis that you may otherwise have made together if you weren't parted?

   a. Such delegation is important as it demonstrates to your ex that you trust them (and should receive such trust back) but it also emphasizes for the kids that there is no checking with Parent B if they don't like what Parent A has said.

   b. Items of greater magnitude should of course still be subject to greater discussion and mutual decision making but it's a good habit to try and act with autonomy and to expect your ex to do the same, otherwise you end up constantly phoning each other when trivial difficulties emerge.

Devolved decision making and presenting a united front in the face of adversity are two further ways in which you can demonstrate to each other, the kids and the world that you are a unified parenting team. You aren't a couple any longer, but you are still a joint parenting team, still focussed on raising your kids jointly, and still keen to enforce the same rules and expectations in spite of the separation that has occurred.

Golden Rule #11

Communication between you and your ex is CRITICAL to the successful maintenance of your shared-parenting. Ensure that you are able to discuss matters in a manner and with due consideration, time and sensitivity depending on the issue at hand.

Key Principles of the Rule

It's becoming a cliché to say that communication is key in virtually all aspects of life. In work, friendship, romantic relationships and the day to day business of going through life, how we communicate with others is pivotal to how successfully we get on with them and what we achieve. The same is true in parenting, and particularly so in shared-parenting.

There's a fundamental barrier to effectively communicating with the other parent of your kids when parenting apart, and the logistics of this are fairly obvious given your shared-history and the fact that at some point you've decided you'd rather live apart. The effectiveness of how you manage in spite of this barrier will be a significant contributing factor to the overall success of your shared-parenting arrangement.

It is of great importance that you ensure that you are able to communicate regularly, effectively and in non-emotive terms if you are able to effectively manage your parenting roles. This may at times be confined to the occasional call or text, sometimes you can cover things off in a 10-minute chat on 'changeover day' and on other occasions you may need to allocate more time and plan a specific meeting date and venue. Whatever it takes, I'm advocating in the strongest terms that you accept you'll need to communicate as effectively, if not more effectively than you did when you were still a couple.

At this point when you're presumably still in the process of splitting or at least the wounds are all still relatively fresh, this must be hard to contemplate. I suggest though that you accept it as a guiding principle and decide if you think it is a realistic prospect for the future.

Questions and considerations for the application of the rule

The following questions and prompts illustrate the considerations you and your ex need to make when contemplating shared-parenting. Some will be best considered by you individually, others by you together.

1) Putting aside all emotional baggage from your relationship, are you willing and able to communicate freely, honestly and regularly with your ex on matters regarding your kids?

    a. This may well have to be prediction of your future intent and willingness to a large extent, if you are still in the midst of splitting up as emotions are doubtless still pretty raw. However, the reality of shared-parenting is that it requires communication from the start, and whilst I accept that this might be a bit begrudging and forced when you've recently parted, you should be striving to be able to communicate effectively on an ongoing basis; this is the critical success factor within this lesson.

2) Are they willing to communicate with you in the same manner?

    a. As willing as you may be, it is not necessarily the case that one person's willingness is reflected in the other. If both of you are in different mental places as far as this is concerned then it hinders the effectiveness of the set-up at least in the first instance and it may well be more appropriate to hold off setting up shared-parenting until such a time as wounds have healed a little.

3) Do you accept that there will be occasions when you need to allocate more time on occasion to meet up with your ex and discuss certain topics in more depth as the need arises?

    a. Not everything can be covered off in a text conversation or a phone call. Email dialogues can be effective, but can become drawn out and sometimes it is easiest to be business-like, draw up an agenda or simple list of things you need to discuss and then to meet up and work through the list. If the set-up of the arrangement has been rigorous and structured then the need for major regular 'summits' on the subject should be limited anyway.

b. Is this potential need accepted by any new partner that you may have? A later chapter touches upon the need to preserve your shared-parenting structure as new relationships are forged and this is covered in depth in the original book. For the purposes of this question though, you and your ex need to retain an ongoing commitment to the structure that you have put in place for the benefit of your kids and the communication between you both cannot be interrupted or interfered with by future partners. I learned this lesson to my significant cost and it is fortunate that several years later our shared-parenting arrangement has survived this threat. You can read more on this in the original book if you wish to.

c. Is this potential need accepted by your wider family and friends? As above, family and friends may also be fearful that you retain frequent and regular contact with your ex and it is important that they recognise this is in the context of and necessary for the maintenance of your shared-parenting structure. If they voice this objection it may be that they need to understand better what you are doing and why and you may find it useful to draw their attention to this book.

4) Can you focus your communications on the neds of your kids rather than any other topics that may arise (such as events from your past)?

a. In a nutshell, keep to the topic at hand.

Shared-parenting doesn't demand that you and your ex put aside all your differences and present a veneer of being best-friends. It's not about righting the wrongs of your marriage or a stepping stone to reconciliation, but it *is* about putting the needs of your kids to the fore and establishing and servicing a structure that does this for the long term. As such, effective and focussed communication between you on topics relating to your kids is essential if you want to make it work.

The conversation doesn't have to be more than polite and business-like (although in my experience as the years go by it becomes easy to be civil and even friendly, and this certainly helps with making it all work effectively). However, it is vital that as with the previous chapter on finances, topics of conversation within the shared-parenting arrangement are constrained to parenting and your kids and detached from wider conversations regarding your failed relationship. That way, the positive and beneficial effects can be felt without drawing out the baggage from the past.

Golden Rule #12

Both of your children's places of residence should feel like and be treated as their homes. This sense should come about through both places being physically decorated to feel like home, with as few of their possessions following them about as possible to encourage a sense of permanence and belonging at both homes. A few basic principles can be adopted to ensure that the transit of 'things' between homes is kept to a minimum

Key Principles of the Rule

In line with the assumptions behind what shared-parenting looks like conceptually, I'm assuming that once set-up, the kids will most likely have two homes where they were previously used to only one. I'm not overly concerned whether one of the two homes was originally the family home pre-divorce, or if one of the two homes is perhaps that of wider family; financial constraints may well decree that initially, the best way shared-parenting can be accommodated is by calling on support from yours or your exes wider family.

If the wider family are having difficulty in buying into the concept of shared-parenting, then please feel free to point them to my book where they can gain a better understanding of the concept and why you are considering it for your separated family as the best solution to meet the needs of your kids.

The fundamental consideration though is that neither one place nor the other should have any hierarchical status over the other as the 'main' home. The kids (and parents) need to adapt to the viewpoint that the children's home is where they are in that moment. A structured arrangement that is repeatable and routine will allow the comfort and familiarity to emerge over time, however the ethos that should be adopted should absolutely be based on both homes being the kids' homes, and that they simply have two bedrooms and so-on where their 'conventional' friends may have only one.

Questions and considerations for the application of the rule

The following questions and prompts illustrate the considerations you and your ex need to make when contemplating shared-parenting. Some will be best considered by you individually, others by you together.

1) If you are remaining in the home that used to be the family-home pre-divorce, are you willing to actively enforce for the kids that yours is just one of their two homes?

   a. It's a subtle distinction, but I've learned through experience that nobody benefits from feeling in any way temporary about where they lay their head at the end of a working (or playing) day. Both your home and that of your ex, regardless of whether one of those two places was formerly the marital family home, should be labelled or treated as the sole 'home'. To seek to label your home as that, for the purposes or perception of your kids will only serve to undermine the home of your ex, and will also undermine the fundamental structure of the arrangement as a whole potentially discouraging them from adapting to the situation and lessening their comfort with the arrangement.

2) Are you financially and emotionally able to equip both homes to an equal or equivalent standard such that neither place is considered sub-standard by the kids?

   a. This isn't a debate over money, since the kids will benefit from a richness of relationships by having both parents actively involved in their lives post-split. However, it's important that both homes actually feel homely, and that the kids can relax and be themselves and feel settled in both locations. In my experience, kids have more than enough 'stuff' which, when divided between two places serves equally to make both homes feel familiar.

   b. In my original book I talk about the importance of there not being a huge volume of 'stuff' that follows the kids around transferring between two homes. It is an inevitability of life that there will be certain school uniforms, musical instruments, favoured toys and gadgets that are both required in both locations and which need to transition between the two homes. However, I advocate (as far as possible and within the bounds of what is financially-feasible) that you should strive for a certain amount of duplication between homes (for example a couple of sets of casual clothes and shoes, toys split between locations and a couple of sets of toiletries etc) in order that the kids don't feel like they're moving home at the start/end of every week.

It is hard to empathise to how this must look from a child's perspective, but I can attest that in 11+ years, having moved home a few times (as has my ex), kids are remarkably resilient and more than that, actually happy to have multiple bedrooms. The novelty factor of being in a different place (once it is also a familiar place) seems to be a positive thing rather than a problem to be weathered. Toys that have been forgotten about or left for a week or more gain new appeal and particularly when they were younger it was apparent that they'd be quite excited about the return to my home after a week away; I'd also hope they were pleased to see me too of course!

The main thing to remember with this, as with all facets of shared-parenting if done in the right way for the right reasons, is that you are acting in your perceived best interests of the kids. Taken as a whole, whilst some circumstances may seem non-ideal to the kids or to onlookers, the reality is that most kids would rather have regular quality time with both their parents rather than a guarantee of one bedroom every night of the year!

Golden Rule #13

It is imperative that you protect and preserve the sanctity and structure of your shared-parenting arrangement as you would protect your kids themselves. Do not allow yourself to be swayed by others be they friends, family, new partners or acquaintances in terms of being forced to modify any aspect unless it is specifically for the benefit of the children. In this case, such changes should be discussed and agreed with the person whom you share the parenting with.

Key Principles of the Rule

At this point in your lives it is natural that your friends and family, your wider circle-of-trust of people who care about you and your kids will be worried for all of you. That is entirely natural and to be expected and as with the other aspects of your split, those close to you who are on 'your side' will want you to come out of your divorce or separation for the better.

What I have observed in this regard as far as shared-parenting is concerned is that many can struggle to understand the motive behind it, that at a point you are finishing a relationship (in some cases those around you may feel that you are actually *escaping* the relationship) it seems odd to them that you are considering a parenting structure that maintains a closer tie with your ex than may traditionally seem necessary.

In the context of the long term future of a shared-parenting arrangement, the purpose of this rule is to act as a reminder of the fact that your actions are driven first and foremost by what you see as the beneficial effects for your kids (golden rule number 1) and doing something that is intended to put their needs to the fore.

I'm guessing that given the choice, certainly at the point of splitting most of us would wish never to have to see our ex again. It is natural to expect that whatever the event that led to the demise of the relationship, there is just cause that has led both parties to deem the relationship to be over and the cleanest split in even the most amicable of break-ups would no doubt be made easier if you never had to encounter your ex in future. As we learn though when we get older, what we would like, and what we consider ideal scenario seldom matches up to what life gives us. The reality is even for those without kids in their relationship they will still likely share a social network, friendship groups, maybe even a work-place where they will need to continue to encounter the other. Both will probably still inhabit the same general town or city.

For those with kids, the inevitability is that you will still face regular interaction with your ex, and in the case of shared-parenting it is a feature rather than a side-effect. If you can elevate yourself to see above the emotional noise and the potentially disparaging views of your friends and family and are contemplating shared-parenting as the means of continuing to both actively involve yourselves in the lives of your kids then you are already a good few steps ahead of those who follow a more traditional model of parenting post-divorce.

What you need to do though at the outset is to be mindful that many others will view the arrangement cynically both for the continuing role it ensures your ex will play in your life, and for the non-traditional approach that you are considering. Most people like and feel comfort with convention and for this reason are generally sceptical and cynical when they see someone contemplating an alternative course of action.

Try and ignore this as a consideration in whether you undertake shared-parenting or not. It is a fine-balance to achieve, and I'm not suggesting you should ignore the views of others, but rather to consider their viewpoint and how this may potentially be influencing what they say. If they express a concern, give it thought but don't reject shared-parenting out of hand just because your parents don't 'get-it' (for example). Do what you think is right for you and your separated family. And if you get further down the line, remain mindful of the potentially limited value that the input of others outside of the arrangement can have.

Questions and considerations for the application of the rule

The following questions and prompts will illustrate the considerations you and your ex need to make when contemplating shared-parenting. Some will be best considered by you individually, others by you together.

1) Can you foresee any basis to the objections that those around you (friends, family, co-workers etc) are voicing to you entering into a shared-parenting arrangement with your ex?

   a. Consider the viewpoint of objectors and whether their perspective is skewed by events from the past - your parents may hate your ex and want them out of your life due to (for example) an infidelity that they committed, but does this warrant the exclusion of them from the lives of your kids if they were a good parent?

   b. Others may simply reject the validity of the arrangement as it doesn't follow the conventional set-up. Others still may have gone down the conventional route (or someone close to them might have) and they may be envious of the fact that you are trying to do it in a different and better way for all involved.

   c. Don't reject advice or guidance offered to you in good faith (I have unfortunately done this a great-deal in my life, often to my cost) but rather take it at face value and explore whether there is genuine value in it or whether the person offering it has a hidden or personal agenda.

2) Can you genuinely contemplate regular communication and interaction with your ex that will be positive and focussed on the commitment you have both made to shared-parenting, putting aside your differences and the causes of your split?

   a. If you can, then chances are that in-spite of objections from others you are destined to prove them wrong.

3) Are you entering into shared-parenting for reasons that are based around the needs of your kids or is this a means of you retaining a tie to your ex?

   a. This is a far-fetched and specific example perhaps, but it maybe signifies the types of reasons that others can concoct for cynically viewing your proposed arrangement.

4) Are you entering into shared-parenting as a means of preserving yours and your extended-families' access to your kids?

   a. This is an intrinsic side-effect to the arrangement in that you should all be able to remain a closer tie than is traditionally experienced, but it shouldn't be the main factor. It is essential that the arrangement as a whole is built around delivering beneficial effects for the kids and to retain a regular visit for grandparents when other aspects of the arrangement might not be favourable is not going to deliver the best for them.

If you are genuinely applying all the golden-rules in evaluating and adopting shared-parenting then you should have a clear-conscience and should be able to fend-off any objections voiced by others.

Envy, fear and ignorance are powerful motivators and outsiders to your shared-parenting set-up may well view it with a mix of these emotions driving their thoughts and responses.

As long as you are convinced you have done it for the right reasons, and in the right way, I advise that you take on board what others say and take from it only that which you genuinely hold to be true.

Golden Rule #14

As you enter into new relationships, and indeed as you contemplate any major life changes, ensure that you are being 100% true to yourself and ensuring that you don't waver on the things that are essential to you in living the life you want. Failing to do this will impact upon your happiness as a person, and on your ability to be the parent that you want to be to your kids.

Key Principles of the Rule

This is the only golden rule that potentially has no real application in the considerations you are making at this stage, since it was derived from my experiences in relationships that followed years after I first divorced, and long after my shared-parenting arrangement had been in place.

I failed to protect my arrangement, allowed my new partner to drive a wedge between me and my ex (in terms of not allowing communication between me and her in relation to our shared-parenting of our kids) and also between my kids and her (effectively ruling out any contact or communication between them and her when they were with us). The relationship in question thankfully came to an end and I'm pleased to say that the terms of the shared-parenting I had previously enjoyed were recovered and retained. I had lost sight though of the need to treat my shared-parenting arrangement as a sacred given in my life that any future partner would need to accept and adapt to, rather than adapting and bending it to accommodate the needs, whims or insecurities on their part.

If you go as far as implementing shared-parenting at some point following your split then of course I hope you may be interested to read more in the full version of my book and the lessons learned in this phase of my life will hopefully serve as a warning to you of the importance of this golden rule.

At this point though, this rule is still perhaps relevant to those whose relationship has parted due to the involvement of a third party. In this instance, I am assuming that one of the parents has left their partner for another person and set up home with them. This puts up a number of additional emotional barriers that may exist and will make a shared-parenting arrangement even harder to establish from the outset unless both parents are particularly sanguine and able to focus solely on the needs of the kids. This is also the main intention in considering shared-parenting as a whole so I won't rule out that this scenario can be made to work, but I contend that it may not be something that is immediately pursued, at least not until the new relationship has been given time and proven to be enduring. In this instance, a more traditional and less 'full-time' visitation may be most appropriate for the parent who has a new partner already.

Questions and considerations for the application of the rule

The following questions and prompts illustrate the considerations you and your ex need to make when contemplating shared-parenting. Some will be best considered by you individually, others by you together.

1) Are you committed to protecting your shared-parenting arrangement as another immovable facet of your life, come what may in your future?

    a. The fact that you have a shared-parenting arrangement for the kids of your failed relationship should be treated as a given just as you treat your job, where you live and your core-beliefs or religion as a part of you and who you are. To consider it as movable, optional or mutable signifies that you aren't as committed to it as is required.

    b. Similarly, if you are entering into a new relationship with someone who is starting to suggest changes are made, or whose insecurities (or other difficulties are indicative of discomfort with the set-up) are starting to cause difficulties in your new relationship, I would suggest that the person may well have emotional baggage from their past which they'd be well advised to deal with before they enter into a relationship with you or anyone else.

2) If you have already entered into a new relationship post-divorce (whether this was part of the reason for your split or not) are you convinced of the long-term future of this relationship sufficiently that you are willing to involve your kids in it?

a. Trying to put aside notions of romance, you need to be certain that your new relationship is solid and will endure before you involve your kids in that, otherwise you run a very real risk of demonstrating to them that your ethos regarding relationships is that they are disposable and not something that you hold any commitment to beyond the short to medium term.

b. In this instance, I suggest a healthier approach would be to respect yourself, your ex, your kids and your new partner and determine if your relationship is truly going to endure, and if so, to then contemplate whether you wish to build a shared-parenting arrangement around that

3) If your ex has a new partner (whether that is someone they parted with you to move in with or whatever other scenario has led to them entering into a new relationship), are you sufficiently comfortable with their new set-up and do you believe in the longevity of it such that you are comfortable that your kids will be exposed to it?

a. I would suggest it is essential that you can communicate in non-emotional terms with both your ex and their new partner if you are going to be able to service and accept a shared-parenting set-up that involves this third-party. If that acceptance and ability to communicate is lacking, then shared-parenting is unlikely to be a viable option due to the inherent insecurity and discord that is likely to underpin many of the interactions between the relevant parties.

4) Are you considering shared-parenting as the long-term parenting structure that will be used to raise your kids, regardless of what changes may come along in future?

a. The underlying assumption should be that whatever happens in your life of that of your ex, that your shared-parenting arrangement will pervade. It is reasonable to assume that you'll both at some point enter into another relationship, you may co-habit, the new partners in

yours or your ex's lives may bring children from past relationships into
that relationship, or new kids may be conceived and born. These are
only examples of one facet that may change in the coming years, and
it's important that conceptually you are both committed to treating
your shared-parenting of the kids from your relationship as a given
part of your lives.

Since I divorced from the mother of my children, we've both had a number of
relationships, both with other people who had kids of their own of various ages and
others who had no kids. We've both co-habited with other people, been engaged to
be married once since (in both instances these never progressed to marriage) and in
separate relationships we've both eventually re-married.

Aside from the difficulties previously mentioned, the shared-parenting arrangement
that we have serviced for in excess of 10 years has pervaded. I mention this to
illustrate that if nothing else, I speak from experience!

My second wife has two kids from a previous marriage whose parenting structure is
more traditional with occasional weekend visitation with their Dad. Whilst our family
model seems to get more complex by the year, this is also mentioned to emphasize
that properly done, shared-parenting is a structure that can be implemented for the
long-term. Kids are for life, after all!

Conclusion

I set out to write this book as a means of distilling some of the key lessons I've learned, and to guide the reader through the considerations and discussions that I feel need to be made at the outset where two parents, soon-to-be separated or divorced from each other are contemplating shared-parenting.

I respect and understand that at the point you are parting, the last thing you need is to have to wade through a hefty book to determine the viability of a lifestyle that you are contemplating for raising your kids. As such I hope this book touches upon the methods that I've found that work in managing the arrangement, but the main focus is upon helping you reach a decision as to whether it is really for you (and your ex) and your kids, or not.

It will come as little surprise that I advocate the system given that I've been driven to assist others in doing the same as me and my ex-wife did. I would like to emphasize though that this is not solely a blinkered viewpoint that has been formulated in isolation; I have had relationships since divorcing in 2006 with those with and without kids, with people who had relationships with their ex's through to those who had taken out restraining orders. I am now married to a fantastic lady whose two kids from her first marriage (who I'm proud to treat as and consider my own) have a relationship with their own father which has followed a more traditional model for a separated family. To that end, they communicate with him little and see him only for odd-weekends. I can assure you it is his loss.

The reason I mention this background is to illustrate that there is some substance to the claims I make as to why shared-parenting is in my view the best way to raise the kids of the separated or divorced family.

When we started the set-up, I had no idea how well it would work, or how well I or the kids would take to it. At the outset of our split, there were numerous reasons (mainly logistical) which dictated that I was more of a weekend Dad for 3 weekends in 4. As such, my ex had the kids Monday to Friday and only for one weekend per month. This arrangement had its benefits and was still arrived at mutually and with consensus, but there was a definite sense of it being an arrangement that wouldn't satisfy any of us in the long term (they were 3 and 6 at the time).

Over time, there have been numerous learnings from and changes made to the setup, but the core principles, summarised as the golden rules in this book and its predecessor remained true and have crystallised in importance.

The situation now is that with two teenage daughters and both my ex and I now married again with marital homes away from where the girls go to school, our innovative approach has continued. We now share a home where the girls are permanently based but into which we (my ex and I) come and go. The property is a 3 bedroomed flat where the girls both have their own bedroom and a third bedroom equipped as a hotel room which is used by the parent of the week. This allows them to feel like they have clarity over where home is, but also that our quality of life is good as well, and none of us feel temporary.

I realise that this isn't perhaps that unusual, but we're certainly the only separated family I'm aware of that does this and as of now it is working well to make the girls feel like they have a single home where they are permanently based (aside from weekend visits to the other homes when appropriate). Essentially though, we're living by the golden rules, most importantly golden rule number 1, where all actions and decisions are based around what is best with the kids.

I strongly advocate shared-parenting as the single best way of meeting the needs of your kids in a separated relationship and I hope that in considering the rules and questions within this book you will be able to reach some informed judgements as to whether it will work for you, your kids and your ex in future.

Whatever path you eventually choose, I would encourage you to keep shared-parenting in mind as a possibility; if it isn't for you now, that may change eventually.

Whatever model you opt for in raising your kids, I wish you a lifetime of happiness and success.

87344357R00043

Made in the USA
Middletown, DE
04 September 2018